and tango makes three

by Justin Richardson and Peter Parnell

illustrated by Henry Cole

Simon & Schuster Books for Young Readers

New York London Toronto Sydney New Delhi

To Gemma—J. R. and P. P.

For KK, with love and admiration—H. C.

SIMON & SCHUSTER BOOKS FOR YOUNG READERS
An imprint of Simon & Schuster Children's Publishing
Division • 1230 Avenue of the Americas, New York, New York
10020 • Text copyright © 2005 by Justin Richardson and Peter
Parnell • Illustrations copyright © 2005 by Henry Cole • All
rights reserved, including the right of reproduction in whole or in
part in any form. • SIMON & SCHUSTER BOOKS FOR YOUNG READERS is a
trademark of Simon & Schuster, Inc. • Book design by Dan Potash •
The text for this book is set in Gararond. • The illustrations for this
book are rendered in watercolor. • Manufactured in China
30 29 28 27 26 25 24 23 22
Library of Congress Cataloging-in-Publication Data • Richardson, Justin,
1963- • And Tango makes three / Justin Richardson and Peter Parnell ;
illustrated by Henry Cole.— 1st ed. • p. cm. • Summary: At New York City's
Central Park Zoo, two male penguins fall in love and start a family by taking turns
sitting on an abandoned egg until it hatches. • ISBN 978-0-689-87845-9
(hardcover) 1. Penguins—Juvenile fiction. [1. Penguins—Fiction. 2. Zoo
animals—Fiction. 3. Familial behavior in animals—Fiction. 4. Homosexuality—
Fiction.] I. Parnell, Peter. II. Cole, Henry, 1955- ill. III. Title.
PZ10.3.R414Tan 2005 • [E]—dc22 2004010176
0515 SCP

With special thanks to Eric Simonoff, David
Gale, Dan Potash, Rob Gramzay, and all our
friends at the Central Park Zoo.—J. R. and P. P.

In the middle of New York City there is a great big park called Central Park. Children love to play there. It has a toy-boat pond where they can sail their boats. It has a carousel to ride on in the summer and an ice rink to skate on in the winter.

Best of all, it has its very own zoo.
Every day families of all kinds go to
visit the animals that live there.

But children and their parents aren't the only families at the zoo. The animals make families of their own. There are red panda bear families, with mothers and fathers and furry red panda bear cubs. There are monkey dads and monkey moms raising noisy monkey babies. There are toad families, and toucan families, and cotton-top tamarin families too.

And in the penguin house there are penguin families.

Every year at the very same time, the girl penguins start noticing the boy penguins. And the boy penguins start noticing the girls. When the right girl and the right boy find each other, they become a couple.

Two penguins in the penguin house were a little bit different.
One was named Roy, and the other was named Silo.
Roy and Silo were both boys. But they did everything together.

They bowed to each other.

And walked together.

They sang to each other.

And swam together.

Wherever Roy went, Silo went too.

They didn't spend much time with the girl penguins, and the girl penguins didn't spend much time with them. Instead, Roy and Silo wound their necks around each other. Their keeper Mr. Gramzay noticed the two penguins and thought to himself, "They must be in love."

Roy and Silo watched how the other penguins made a home.
So they built a nest of stones for themselves. Every night Roy
and Silo slept there together, just like the other penguin couples.

And every morning Roy and Silo woke up together. But one day Roy and Silo saw that the other couples could do something they could not.

The mama penguin would lay an egg. She and the papa penguin would take turns keeping the egg warm until finally, it would hatch. And then there would be a baby penguin.

Roy and Silo had no egg to sit on and keep warm.
They had no baby chick to feed and cuddle and love.
Their nest was nice, but it was a little empty.

One day Roy found something that looked like what the other penguins were hatching and he brought it to their nest.

It was only a rock,

but Silo carefully sat on it.

And sat. . . .

And sat.

When Silo got sleepy, he slept. And when Silo was done sleeping and sitting,
he swam and Roy sat. Day after day Silo and Roy sat on the rock.

But nothing happened.

Then Mr. Gramzay got an idea.

He found an egg that needed to be cared for,
and he brought it to Roy and Silo's nest.

Roy and Silo knew just what to do. They moved the egg to the center of their nest. Every day they turned it, so each side stayed warm. Some days Roy sat while Silo went for food. Other days it was Silo's turn to take care of their egg.

They sat in the morning, and they sat at night.
They sat through lunchtime and swim time and supper.

They sat at the beginning of the month, and they sat at the
end of the month, and they sat all of the days in between.

Until one day they heard a sound coming from inside their egg.
Peep, peep. Peep, peep, it said.
Roy and Silo called back, *Squawk, squawk.*
Peep, peep, answered the egg.

Suddenly a tiny hole appeared in the egg's shell.
And then . . .

CRAAAACK!

Out came their very own baby! She had fuzzy white feathers and a funny black beak. Now Roy and Silo were fathers. "We'll call her Tango," Mr. Gramzay decided, "because it takes two to make a Tango."

Roy and Silo taught Tango how to sing for them when she was hungry. They fed her food from their beaks. They snuggled her in their nest at night.

Tango was the very first penguin in the zoo to have two daddies.

Soon Tango grew strong enough to leave the nest. Roy and Silo took her for a swim, just like all the other penguin families.

And all the children who came to the zoo could see Tango and her two fathers playing in the penguin house with the other penguins.

"Hooray, Roy!" "Hooray, Silo!" "Welcome, Tango!" they cheered.

At night the three penguins returned to their nest.

There they snuggled together and, like all the other penguins in the penguin house, and all the other animals in the zoo, and all the families in the big city around them, they went to sleep.

AUTHORS' NOTE

All of the events in this story are true. Roy and Silo are called chinstrap penguins because of the delicate line of black feathers that loops under their beaks, as if to hold a hat in place. After years of living side by side in the Central Park Zoo, they discovered each other in 1998 and they have been a couple ever since. Tango, their only chick, was born from an egg laid by another penguin couple named Betty and Porkey. That couple had often hatched their own eggs, but they had never been able to care for more than one at a time. In 2000, when Betty laid two fertile eggs, Rob Gramzay decided to give Roy, Silo, and one of those eggs a chance to become a family.

If you go to the Central Park Zoo, you can see Tango and her parents splashing about in the penguin house along with their friends, including Nipper, Squawk, Charlie, Wasabi, and Piwi. There are forty-two chinstrap penguins in the Central Park Zoo and over ten million chinstraps in the world.

But there is only one Tango.

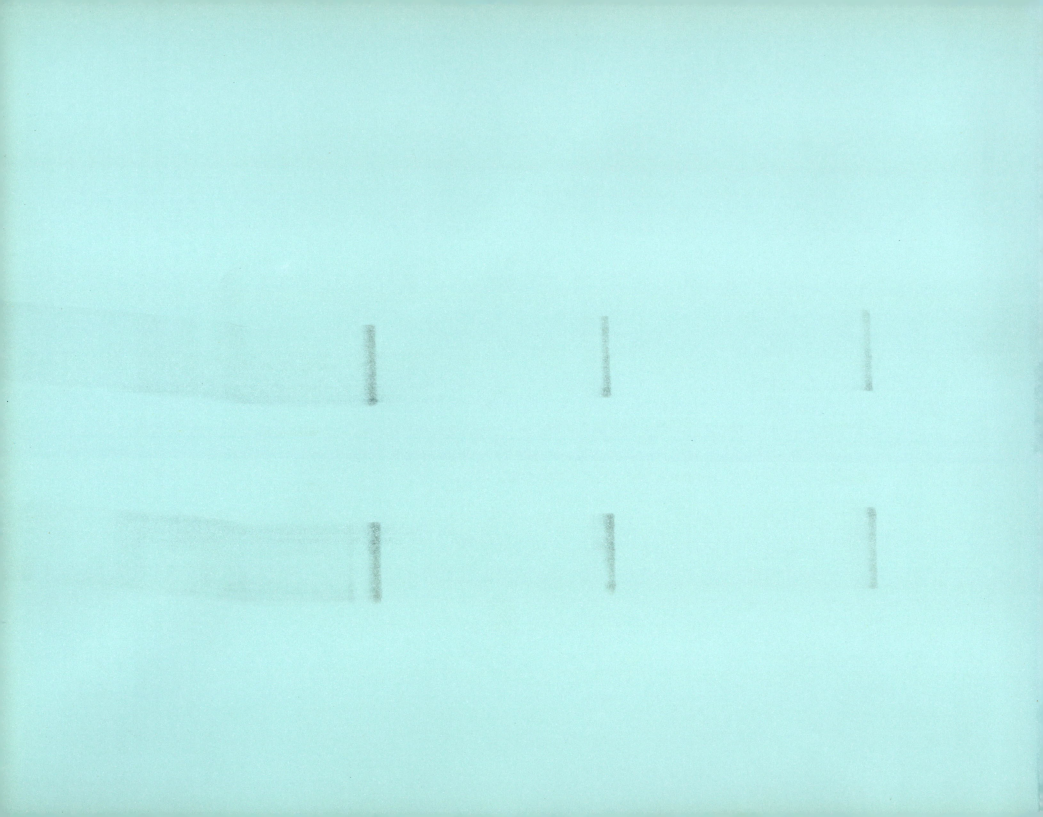